MW01013598

Joseph Haydn

London Symphonies
Nos. 93–98
in Full Score

DOVER PUBLICATIONS, INC.
Mineola, New York

Published in Canada by General Publishing Company, Ltd., 30 Lesmill Road,
Don Mills, Toronto, Ontario.

Bibliographical Note

This Dover edition, first published in 1997, is an unabridged republication of an
authoritative edition, n.d., adding new lists of contents and instrumentation.

International Standard Book Number: 0-486-29754-3

Manufactured in the United States of America
Dover Publications, Inc., 31 East 2nd Street, Mineola, N.Y. 11501

Contents

Instrumentation

2 Flutes [Flauti, Fl.]
2 Oboes [Oboi, Ob.]
2 Bassoons [Fagotti, Fag.]

2 Horns [Corni, Cor.]
2 Trumpets [Trombe, Tr-be]

Timpani [Timpani, Timp.]

Strings [Archi]:
Violins I, II [Violini, V-ni]
Violas [Viole, V-le]
Cellos & Basses [Violoncelli e Contrabassi;
V-celli/o (Vc.) e C-bassi (Cb.)]

London Symphonies
Nos. 93–98

transitions must modulate
what gets developed
closing section at end of expo? coda?

Symphony No. 93 in D Major

(1791)

I

EXPOSITION

Allegro assai

Allegro assai THEME I

I   First key area   V I

new dynamic + winds

new area

transition

2 second theme / key area

Symphony No. 93 (I)   5

transition back to closing section

Cor.

Tr-be

Timp.

fragments string/winds

develop 2nd theme

running 8th note figures derived from closing theme

develop 1st theme

1st & 2nd themes released- monoshematic model

II

Largo cantabile

70

III
Menuetto

Trio

Menuetto da capo

IV
Finale

Symphony No. 93 (*IV*)

Symphony No. 94 in G Major

("The Surprise"; 1791)

I

theme & variations?

Development

RECAP (theme)
I

5

150

2nd theme

+ theme & variation

II

67

Maggiore

70

Fl.
Ob.
Fag.

80

III
Menuetto

IV
Finale

82

Symphony No. 95 in C Minor
(1791)

I

transition to second key

Cor.

DEVELOPMENT

Fl.

Ob.

Fag.

Cor.

Tr-be

Timp.

RECAP

theme 1

Maggiore

140

160

II

Symphony No. 95 (II)

118   *Symphony No. 95* (**II**)

III
Menuetto

IV
Finale

Symphony No. 96 in D Major

("The Miracle"; 1791)

I

Exposition

Allegro

Allegro theme1

144   Symphony No. 96 (I)

development

200

II

Symphony No. 96 (II)

III
Menuetto

173

Menuetto da capo

178   *Symphony No. 96* (**III**)

IV
Finale

179

Symphony No. 97 in C Major
(1792)

I

60

skewing ♭ II 6
(usually cadential)

Coda acts like
2nd development
(closing section)
transition to I

Closing Section - melds into coda

reprise of opening material

II

Adagio ma non troppo THEME

FM

VARIATION 2

126 a2

7 VARIATION 7

131

130

222   Symphony No. 97 (**II**)

Trio

Menuetto da capo

sonata-
rendo

IV
Finale

231

Symphony No. 98 in B-flat Major
(1792)

110

DEVELOPMENT

Fl.

Ob.

Fag.

320

II

Adagio cantabile

Flauto

2 Oboi

2 Fagotti

2 Corni (F)

Adagio cantabile

Violini I

Violini II

Viole

Violoncelli
e Contrabassi

Symphony No. 98 (**II**)   277

III
Menuetto

280

IV
Finale

286

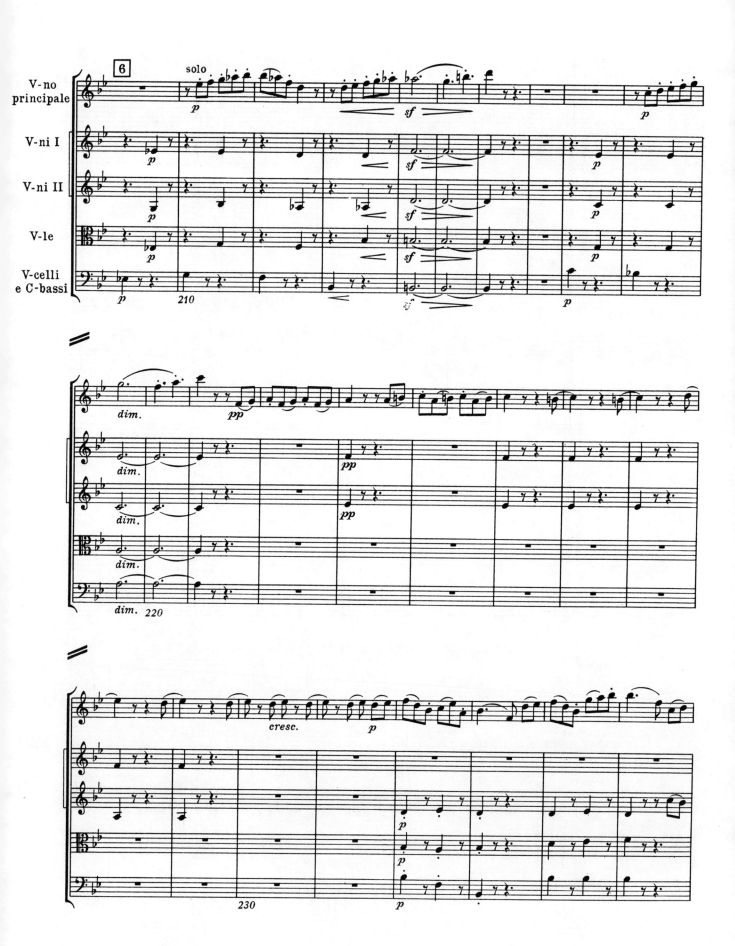

340

END OF EDITION

308   *Symphony No. 98 (IV)*